INSIDE THE CHICAGO CUBS

JON M. FISHMAN

Lerner Publications ◆ Minneapolis

Copyright © 2022 by Lerner Publishing Group, Inc.

All rights reserved. International copyright secured. No part of this book may be reproduced, stored in a retrieval system, or transmitted in any form or by any means—electronic, mechanical, photocopying, recording, or otherwise—without the prior written permission of Lerner Publishing Group, Inc., except for the inclusion of brief quotations in an acknowledged review.

Lerner Publications Company
An imprint of Lerner Publishing Group, Inc.
241 First Avenue North
Minneapolis, MN 55401 USA

For reading levels and more information, look up this title at www.lernerbooks.com.

Main body text set in Aptifer Slab LT Pro / Typeface provided by Linotype AG.

Designer: Kimberly Morales

Library of Congress Cataloging-in-Publication Data

Names: Fishman, Jon M., author.
Title: Inside the Chicago Cubs / Jon M. Fishman.
Description: Minneapolis : Lerner Publications, 2022. | Series: Super sports teams | Includes bibliographical references and index. | Audience: Ages 7–11 | Audience: Grades 2–3 | Summary: "Take the field with the Chicago Cubs in this thrilling title. Learn how the Cubs won three World Series championships and read about their stunning stats, biggest moments, and greatest stars"— Provided by publisher.
Identifiers: LCCN 2021016805 (print) | LCCN 2021016806 (ebook) | ISBN 9781728441733 (library binding) | ISBN 9781728449456 (paperback) | ISBN 9781728445182 (ebook)
Subjects: LCSH: Chicago Cubs (Baseball team)—History—Juvenile literature.
Classification: LCC GV875.C6 F57 2022 (print) | LCC GV875.C6 (ebook) | DDC 796.357/640977311—dc23

LC record available at https://lccn.loc.gov/2021016805
LC ebook record available at https://lccn.loc.gov/2021016806

Manufactured in the United States of America
1-49928-49771-8/16/2021

TABLE OF CONTENTS

BACK ON TOP **4**

BEATING THE CURSE **9**

AMAZING MOMENTS **15**

CUBS SUPERSTARS **21**

MEMORY MAKERS **25**

Cubs Season Record Holders 28
Glossary................................ 30
Learn More 31
Index 32

Dexter Fowler runs around the bases after hitting a home run for the Chicago Cubs during the 2016 World Series.

BACK

FACTS AT A GLANCE

- **THE CUBS** have won the World Series three times.
- **ERNIE BANKS** hit 512 home runs for the Cubs.
- **KRIS BRYANT** is the only player to hit three home runs and two doubles in one game.
- **WRIGLEY FIELD** is the second-oldest Major League Baseball (MLB) ballpark.

Nothing in MLB is more exciting than Game 7 of the World Series. Two teams go toe-to-toe for the championship title. In 2016, the Chicago Cubs had a chance to win the World Series for the first time in more than 100 years. They just had to beat the Cleveland Indians in Game 7.

In the first inning, Dexter Fowler led off for the Cubs. On the fourth pitch of the game, he smacked the ball deep to center field. Cleveland outfielder Rajai Davis leaped and reached over the outfield wall, but he couldn't catch the ball. Home run! Fowler's blast was the first leadoff home run ever hit in Game 7 of the World Series.

The Cubs kept scoring. In the sixth inning, David Ross's home run gave Chicago a 6–3 lead. But in the eighth, Cleveland came storming back. They scored three runs to tie the game.

Game 7 was still tied after nine innings. In the 10th, Chicago's Ben Zobrist hit a double to drive in a run. Then Miguel Montero hit a single to score again. With a two-run lead, the Cubs needed only three outs to win. When Cleveland batted, they put up a tough fight but couldn't catch the Cubs. Chicago won 8–7. They were World Series champions!

The Cubs are one of the most popular teams in MLB. They have fans all around the United States and the world. But for many years, the team didn't have much success. Some fans even thought the team was cursed.

Montero hits an RBI single in Game 7.

Cubs players celebrate winning the World Series.

The Cubs have played at Wrigley Field since 1926.

8

BEATING THE CURSE

The Chicago Cubs are one of the oldest teams in MLB. They have existed longer than the league has. When the team formed in 1870, they were called the Chicago White Stockings.

The White Stockings played in the National Association. In 1876, the White Stockings joined the new National League (NL). The NL was the top pro baseball league in the US.

The 1888 Chicago White Stockings

In 1890, the White Stockings changed their nickname to the Colts. Then they became the Orphans in 1898. Five seasons later, baseball underwent big changes.

The Western League, a minor league, started in 1894. After six seasons, it changed its name to the American League (AL). In 1901, the AL became a major league to compete with the NL. The leagues joined in 1903 to form MLB. That year, the AL-champion Boston Americans beat the NL's Pittsburgh Pirates in the first World Series.

The Orphans had a lot of young players. A Chicago newspaper began calling the team the Cubs in honor of the youngsters. The nickname's popularity grew. In 1907, they officially became the Chicago Cubs.

By then, the team's young players were ready to win. The Cubs had lost the World Series to the Chicago White Sox the year before.

The 1902 Orphans finished fifth in the NL.

Frank Chance bats for the Cubs during the 1907 World Series.

CUBS FACT

Cubs are young meat-eating animals such as bears, foxes, or lions. The Chicago Cubs have images of bears in some of their team logos.

But in 1907, the Cubs crushed the Detroit Tigers in four games. They were MLB champions!

The Cubs returned to the World Series in 1908 against Detroit. Once again, the Tigers were no match for the Cubs. Chicago won the series 4–1 for their second straight MLB title. In 1910, the Cubs fell to the Philadelphia Athletics in the World Series. The loss marked the beginning of a period of bad luck.

Since 1893, the Cubs had played their home games at Chicago's West Side Grounds. That changed after a group led by Charles

Weeghman bought the team. He built Weeghman Park in 1914 and moved the Cubs there in 1916.

The new ballpark didn't change Chicago's luck in the World Series. The Boston Red Sox beat them in 1918. In 1926, after another ownership change, Weeghman Park became Wrigley Field. But the team's bad luck remained. They lost the World Series in 1929, 1932, 1935, and 1938.

The Cubs had another chance to win the MLB championship in 1945. But during the World Series, legend says the team was struck by a so-called curse. Cubs fan William Sianis bought tickets to Game 4

This postcard shows the Cubs playing at Weeghman Park in the 1920s.

Roy Hughes (*bottom center*) crosses home plate to score a run for the Cubs during the 1945 World Series.

for himself and his goat Murphy. When Sianis and Murphy arrived at Wrigley Field, team officials wouldn't let them inside. They said Murphy stunk.

Sianis was outraged. As he left Wrigley with Murphy, he said the Cubs would no longer be a winning team. Chicago lost the World Series to Detroit. Some fans said the Curse of the Billy Goat was the reason.

Curses aren't real, but it was an easy excuse for the team's misfortunes. Decades passed, and the Cubs failed to return to the World Series. In 2008, the team marked the 100-year anniversary of their last MLB championship.

Finally, the Cubs reached the World Series in 2016. When they beat Cleveland, many fans celebrated the end of Sianis's curse. They hoped the victory marked the beginning of a period of success.

Sammy Sosa had a lot of amazing moments in his 13 seasons with the Cubs.

AMAZING MOMENTS

With almost 150 seasons in the NL, the Cubs have many great moments. The team has far too many highlights to cover all of them. One moment that fans will never forget almost didn't happen.

The 1938 Pirates had led the NL for most of the summer. As the season wound down, the Cubs stepped up. Beginning in late August, Chicago won 19 of the 24 games they played. On September 28, the Cubs faced the Pirates in Chicago. They trailed Pittsburgh by 0.5 games in the standings.

Cubs catcher Gabby Harnett practices batting in 1938. That season, he finished second on the team with 10 home runs.

CUBS FACT

Fans call Hartnett's blast the Homer in the Gloamin'. *Gloaming* means "twilight."

Wrigley Field didn't have stadium lights. That meant games couldn't continue after sunset. The game was tied in the bottom of the ninth inning, but it was 5:30 p.m. Sunset was at 5:37.

The umpires talked. It was getting hard to see, but they decided to continue the game and let the Cubs bat. With two outs in the inning, Gabby Hartnett hit for Chicago. He smacked the ball toward left field.

In the twilight, many fans couldn't see the ball. But they saw Pittsburgh's left fielder look up as it flew over the wall. The Cubs celebrated the home run that gave them the NL lead.

Fans rush onto the field after Hartnett's 1938 home run.

Ernie Banks smashes a home run in 1970.

In 1970, Chicago celebrated another great moment. On May 12, first baseman Ernie Banks and the Cubs faced the Atlanta Braves. Banks had 499 career home runs.

Banks was 39 and near the end of his career, but he still had a powerful swing. He smashed a blast over the left-field wall for his 500th home run. Fans at Wrigley cheered as Banks circled the bases.

Almost 30 years later, Cubs fans celebrated another home run hitter. In 1998, Chicago outfielder Sammy Sosa challenged MLB's single-season home run record of 61. Sosa and Mark McGwire of the St. Louis Cardinals put on a home run show.

Kerry Wood had 233 strikeouts in 1998.

Sosa collected 158 RBIs in 1998.

In September, Sosa hit number 62. He ended the season with 66 homers, four fewer than McGwire hit. Fans later learned that Sosa, McGwire, and other MLB players had used steroids, or performance-enhancing drugs (PEDs). At the time, may pro baseball players used PEDs to get stronger and recover quickly from injuries.

Cubs fans also saw an incredible pitching performance in 1998. Chicago faced the Houston Astros at Wrigley on May 6. Cubs pitcher Kerry Wood struck out the first five batters he faced. He was just getting started.

Wood kept striking out Astros batters. In the eighth, he recorded his 16th strikeout to set a new Cubs record. Wood finished the game with 20 strikeouts, the most in NL history. Some baseball fans say it was the greatest pitching performance ever.

In his first eight seasons with the Cubs, pitcher Kyle Hendricks won almost 100 games.

CUBS SUPERSTARS

Cubs fans always have superstars to cheer for. One of the first was Cap Anson, who played for the team from 1876 to 1897. Anson led the NL in batting average twice and in RBIs eight times. When he retired, he led the NL in career hits, doubles, and runs.

Ernie Banks retired with 512 home runs, tied for 23rd in MLB history. He played all of his 19 MLB seasons with Chicago. That's one reason fans called him Mr. Cub.

Banks watches a home run soar over the outfield wall.

Ryne Sandberg was one of the best second basemen ever. Playing for the Cubs from 1982 to 1997, Sandberg wowed fans with his bat and his glove. He set a record for most games in a row at second base without an error (123). When he retired, he held the all-time record for most home runs as a second baseman (277).

Sammy Sosa's 609 career home runs are the ninth most by any player. Cubs fans loved his high-energy style and broad smile. But many also think he cheated by using steroids. That's one reason he hasn't been elected to the Baseball Hall of Fame.

Sandberg was named the best second baseman in the NL nine times in a row.

CUBS FACT

In 2016, Cubs slugger Kris Bryant became the first MLB player to hit three home runs and two doubles in a game.

Cubs fans cheer after Willson Contreras catches the ball for an out.

In the 2020s, the Cubs are packed with talent. Kyle Hendricks and new star Adbert Alzolay lead the team's pitchers. Sluggers Willson Contreras and Ian Happ blast long home runs and rack up RBIs. Cubs fans have a lot to be excited about.

Wrigley Field is located in Chicago's North Side community.

MEMORY MAKERS

By 1948, every MLB ballpark had lights for night games except one: Wrigley Field. Unlike other teams, the Cubs played all their games during the day. The team finally added lights in 1988. The first night game occurred on August 8. The Cubs beat the New York Mets 6–4.

Wrigley Field is the second-oldest MLB ballpark behind Boston's Fenway Park. Wrigley isn't as comfortable as many modern stadiums. It has bleachers in the outfield instead of seats. Some fans have to look around poles and other objects to see the field.

Fans enjoy the first night game at Wrigley Field.

Despite missing some modern comforts, no ballpark has more charm than Wrigley. The brick outfield walls are covered in green ivy. Across the street, fans line rooftops to watch the action. They can see players hitting and throwing on the same field where Ernie Banks, Ryne Sandberg, and many others became legends.

The Cubs haven't returned to the World Series since 2016. But fans no longer joke about the team being cursed. Win or lose, going to a ball game at Wrigley is one of the best experiences in sports. For over 150 years, the Cubs have been a source of joy and fun. Fans look forward to many more years of memories.

Ian Happ jumps against Wrigley's outfield wall for a catch.

Cubs fans are eager for another World Series win.

CUBS SEASON RECORD HOLDERS

Sammy Sosa

HITS
1. Rogers Hornsby, 229 (1929)
2. Kiki Cuyler, 228 (1930)
3. Billy Herman, 227 (1935)
4. Woody English, 214 (1930)
5. Frank Demaree, 212 (1936)

HOME RUNS
1. Sammy Sosa, 66 (1998)
2. Sammy Sosa, 64 (2001)
3. Sammy Sosa, 63 (1999)
4. Hack Wilson, 56 (1930)
5. Sammy Sosa, 50 (2000)

RBIS
1. Hack Wilson, 191 (1930)
2. Sammy Sosa, 160 (2001)
3. Hack Wilson, 159 (1929)
4. Sammy Sosa, 158 (1998)
5. Rogers Hornsby, 149 (1929)

WINS
1. John Clarkson, 53 (1885)
2. Al Spalding, 47 (1876)
3. Bill Hutchison, 44 (1891)
4. Larry Corcoran, 43 (1880)
5. Bill Hutchison, 41 (1890)

STRIKEOUTS
1. Bill Hutchison, 314 (1892)
2. John Clarkson, 313 (1886)
3. John Clarkson, 308 (1885)
4. Bill Hutchison, 289 (1890)
5. Fergie Jenkins, 274 (1970)

SAVES
1. Randy Myers, 53 (1993)
2. Rod Beck, 51 (1998)
3. Carlos Marmol, 38 (2010)
   Randy Myers, 38 (1995)
5. Bruce Sutter, 37 (1979)

GLOSSARY

blast: a home run

curse: a misfortune that comes in response to something

double: a hit in baseball that allows the batter to reach second base

lead off: to bat first for a team in an inning

major league: the highest league in pro baseball

minor league: a pro baseball league that is not a major league

pro: short for professional, taking part in an activity to make money

RBI: a run in baseball that is driven in by a batter

single: a hit in baseball that allows the batter to reach first base

umpire: a baseball official who rules on plays

LEARN MORE

Chicago Cubs
https://www.mlb.com/cubs

Chicago Cubs History
https://www.mlb.com/cubs/history

Flynn, Brendan. *Chicago Cubs All-Time Greats*. Burnsville, MN: Press Box Books, 2021.

Monson, James. *Behind the Scenes Baseball*. Minneapolis: Lerner Publications, 2020.

National Baseball Hall of Fame
https://baseballhall.org/

Whiting, Jim. *The Story of the Chicago Cubs*. Mankato, MN: Creative Education, 2021.

INDEX

Banks, Ernie, 17, 21, 26

Chicago White Stockings, 9–10

Curse of the Billy Goat, 13

home run, 5, 16–17, 21–23

Montero, Miguel, 6

National League (NL), 9–10, 15–16, 19, 21

Sianis, William, 12–13

Sosa, Sammy, 17, 19

stadium lights, 16

Weeghman Park, 12

Wood, Kerry, 19

World Series, 5–6, 10–13, 26

Wrigley Field, 12–13, 16–17, 19, 25–26

PHOTO ACKNOWLEDGMENTS

Image credits: Gene Puskar/Pool/Getty Images, p. 4; Ezra Shaw/Getty Images, p. 6; Cal Sport Media via AP Images, p. 7; smontgom65/iStock/Getty Images, p. 8; Library of Congress (LC-DIG-ppmsca-18835), p. 9; George R Lawrence/Wikimedia Commons (public domain), p. 10; The Rucker Archive/Icon Sportswire/Getty Images, p. 11; Mark Rucker/Transcendental Graphics/Getty Images, p. 12; Bettmann/Getty Images, p. 13; PCN Photography/Alamy Stock Photo, p. 14; Bruce Bennett/Getty Images, p. 15; Chicago Daily News Inc./Chicago History Museum/Getty Images, p. 16; AP Photo/Warren Wimmer, p. 17; Harry How/Allsport/Getty Images, p. 18; David Durochik via AP, p. 19; Todd Kirkland/Getty Images, p. 20; Hy Peskin Archive/Getty Images, p. 21; Ronald C. Modra/Getty Images, p. 22; Jon Durr/Getty Images, p. 23; Marco Verch/flickr (CC BY 2.0), p. 24; Paul Natkin/Getty Images, p. 25; Brian Cassella/Chicago Tribune/TNS/Alamy Stock Photo, p. 26; Patrick Gorski/Icon Sportswire/Getty Images, p. 27; Sporting News/Getty Images, p. 28.

Design element: Master3D/Shutterstock.com.

Cover: Rob Tringali/MLB/Getty Images.

WITHDRAWN